FAMOUS

Poem by Naomi Shihab Nye

Illustrations by Lisa Desimini

✯ Wings Press ✯
San Antonio, Texas

Famous © 2015
by Wings Press
for Naomi Shihab Nye (text) and Lisa Desimini (illustrations)

ISBN: 978-1-60940-449-9 (Hardback)

E-books:

ePub: 978-1-60940-450-5
Mobipocket/Kindle: 978-1-60940-451-2
Library PDF: 978-1-60940-452-9

Wings Press
627 E. Guenther
San Antonio, Texas 78210
Phone/fax: (210) 271-7805
On-line catalogue and ordering:
www.wingspress.com

Wings Press books are distributed to the trade by
Independent Publishers Group
www.ipgbook.com

Library of Congress Cataloging-in-Publication Data:

Nye, Naomi Shihab.
  Famous : poem / by Naomi Shihab Nye ; illustrations by Lisa Desimini.
    pages cm
ISBN 978-1-60940-449-9 (hardback/cloth : alk. paper) -- ISBN 978-1-
60940-450-5 (e-pub ebook) -- ISBN 978-1-60940-451-2 (mobipocket/
kindle ebook) -- ISBN 978-1-60940-452-9 (library pdf)
  I. Desimini, Lisa, illustrator. II. Title.
  PS3564.Y44F36 2015
  811'.54--dc23
                            2015005174

Printed in China

To your secret shining self.
And to anyone who thinks
nobody notices them.

The river is famous

to the fish.

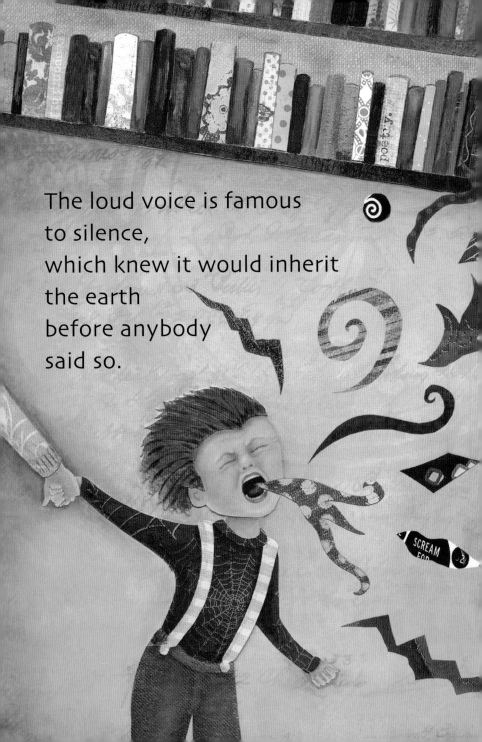

The loud voice is famous
to silence,
which knew it would inherit
the earth
before anybody
said so.

The cat sleeping on the fence
is famous to the birds
watching him from the birdhouse.

The tear is famous, briefly,
to the cheek.

The idea you carry
close to your heart
is famous to your heart.

The boot is famous to the earth,
more famous than the dress shoe,

which is famous only to floors.

The bent photograph is famous
to the one who carries it,
not at all famous
to the one who is pictured.

famous as the one who smiled back.

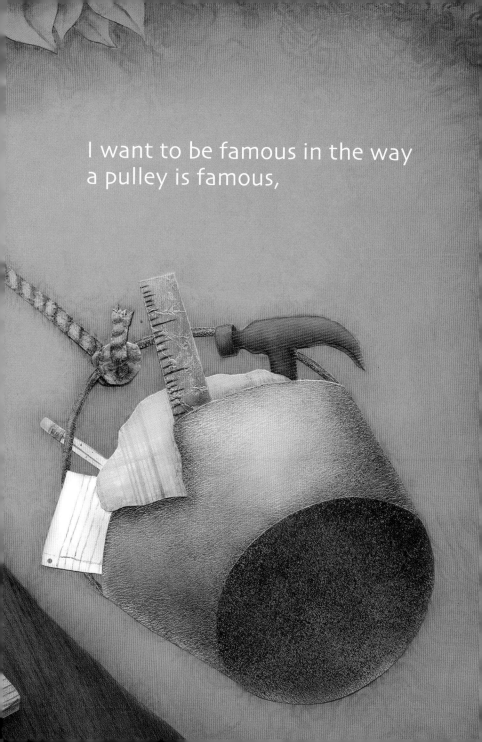

I want to be famous in the way
a pulley is famous,

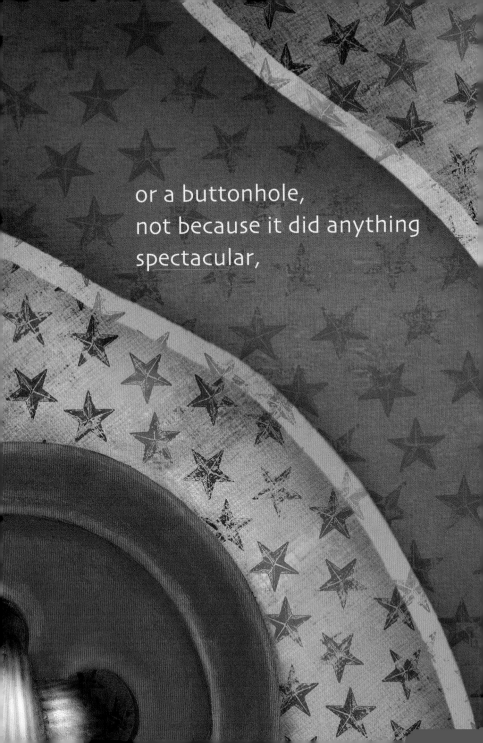

or a buttonhole,
not because it did anything
spectacular,

but because
it never forgot
what it could do.

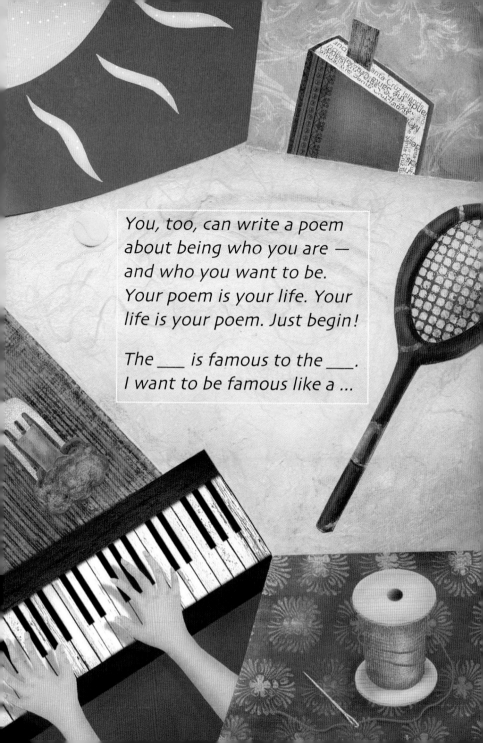

You, too, can write a poem about being who you are — and who you want to be. Your poem is your life. Your life is your poem. Just begin!

The ___ is famous to the ___.
I want to be famous like a ...

WingsPress

Publishing fine multicultural literature since 1975.

www.wingspress.com

Book design by Bryce Milligan.